JAMES COOK
Changing the Map of the World

by Cynthia Clampitt

Editorial Offices: Glenview, Illinois • Parsippany, New Jersey • New York, New York

Sales Offices: Needham, Massachusetts • Duluth, Georgia • Glenview, Illinois
Coppell, Texas • Ontario, California • Mesa, Arizona

Explorer of the World

In the mid-1700s, people in the **Northern Hemisphere** knew very little about the **Southern Hemisphere**. Between 1768 and 1779 James Cook changed that. In fact, Cook changed the map of the world more than any other person in history. His **voyages** took him all over the world, although he is probably best known for his explorations south of the **equator**.

Cook became famous for more than just his explorations, however. He wrote thousands of pages about the lands, plants, and animals he and his men discovered and the people they met. He was an artist who sketched the things he saw. He was a scientist who studied the Sun and planets. He also studied health and nutrition, which helped him discover a way to prevent **scurvy**. Scurvy is a disease caused by a lack of vitamin C, and it was the number one cause of death on long voyages in the 1700s. Cook's skill in mathematics helped him create charts and maps of great accuracy. He was respected by the men who sailed with him.

Capt. James Cook spent most of his adult life sailing the world's oceans.

The thing that surprised most people in Cook's day was that James Cook was not from a rich or powerful family. Most well-known leaders at that time were from the upper class. In fact, James Cook's family was quite poor. To become a captain, he had to work harder than other officers in the British navy.

Cook was intelligent and courageous, a hard worker, and passionate about learning. These qualities earned him respect—and they led him on the long voyages he would take to explore worlds unknown to him. He is still considered by many to be the world's greatest explorer.

Cook's Early Years

James Cook was born in a small farming village in northern England. His father was a poor farmworker from Scotland. A farmer who hired his father noticed how smart James was, so the farmer offered to send James to school. From the age of eight to the age of twelve, James studied reading, writing, and arithmetic. He still helped his father on the farm, but he spent all of his free time studying.

When Cook was sixteen, he got a job at a store in a village near Whitby, a busy port filled with ships. Cook was a good worker, but the shopkeeper could see that Cook was interested in the ships. After a year and a half, the shopkeeper introduced Cook to a ship owner in Whitby. Cook's life at sea had begun.

James Cook was born in a cottage in northern England on October 27, 1728, similar to this one.

It was here, in the English town of Whitby, that Cook first came in contact with ships and the sea.

Cook spent the next eight years learning about ships and sailing. The Whitby ships sailed the dangerous waters of the North Sea. Learning to sail there equipped Cook to sail anywhere. During the winter, Cook studied mathematics, geography, and astronomy, the study of stars and planets.

Cook was promoted many times as his skills and knowledge grew. He also grew in height and was now more than six feet tall. He was offered another promotion, but he wanted more than the North Sea shippers offered. He decided that the British navy would give him more opportunities to see the world.

The Royal Navy

Life in the Royal Navy was not easy. Ships were crowded and trips were long. Many men died of scurvy. Cook did not like everything he saw, but he obeyed orders, worked hard, and was quickly promoted. Every chance he had, he continued his studies. He knew the life he wanted would require much knowledge.

Soon Cook had command of his own ship. The Seven Years' War had begun, and Cook was sent to defend the northern coast of England. Then, in 1757 he was ordered to Canada. There he met a man who taught him the science of surveying, which is the careful measuring of the size, shape, and location of places.

The Seven Years' War

The Seven Years' War lasted from 1756 to 1763. It involved all of the major European powers of that time. While much of the war took place in Europe, the part of it that was fought in North America is known in the United States as the French and Indian War. The French and Indian War began in 1754.

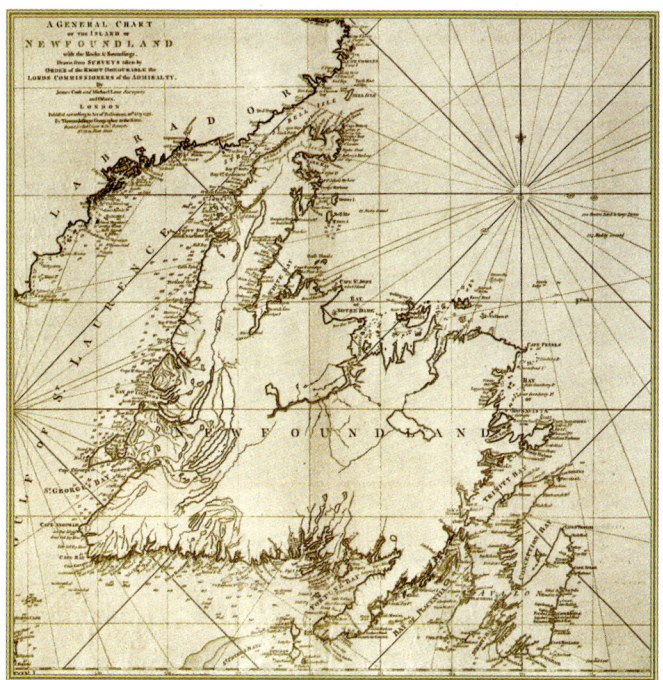

James Cook learned to make accurate, detailed maps, such as this one of Newfoundland.

Surveying was a new science, but Cook realized that it would become an important one. He studied hard and was soon a skilled surveyor. This skill soon proved to be very useful. Cook's survey of the St. Lawrence River helped General Wolfe's army land safely at Quebec, where they won Canada for Britain.

Cook soon found himself assigned to surveying full-time. From 1763 to 1768, Cook spent his summers surveying eastern Canada and his winters creating maps in England. But it was his scientific reports that made people begin to take notice of him. Most naval officers didn't write about the Sun and the planets!

The First Voyage of Discovery

A group of British scientists needed someone for a special project. This person would have to go to the far side of the Earth and observe the planet Venus passing in front of the Sun. Using this information, the scientists would be able to mathematically calculate the distance between Earth and the Sun. A ship's captain who was also an astronomer and mathematician would be the perfect person for such a task.

In August 1768 James Cook set sail in a ship called the *Endeavour*. Remembering the things he did not like about his early days in the Royal Navy, Cook insisted on cleanliness and a healthful diet. He felt certain that if his men ate right, they would not die of scurvy.

In Tahiti people paddled their canoes out to greet Cook's ship. Detailed drawings such as this one show us what Cook and his crew saw as they traveled.

This stamp from 1940 shows Cook; his ship, the *Endeavour*; and his chart of New Zealand.

Cook went first to Tahiti, where he and another scientist made the needed measurements of the movements of the planet Venus. Then he opened a new set of orders. He was told to explore the southern **latitudes**, to determine if there was another continent south of the equator.

Cook found and charted New Zealand, a difficult task that took six months. Heading west, he arrived at the east coast of Australia. Sailing north, he charted the 2,000-mile-long coast as well. Many discoveries were made. The botanists, or plant scientists, on the voyage identified so many new plants in one place that Cook named the spot Botany Bay.

Finally, in 1771 the *Endeavour* headed back toward England. All of Cook's accomplishments were important, but there was one real surprise: in three years at sea, Cook had not lost anyone to scurvy. This had never happened before. Cook's ideas about health and diet had been correct.

The Second Voyage

Many people in the 1700s believed that there must be another continent in the Southern Hemisphere. Also, while latitude had been measured, longitude had never been measured accurately. Again, an explorer was needed who was also a mathematician and a scientist. Cook had only been home for one year when he was asked to go on another voyage.

Cook departed in July 1772. He took with him the first clock that would work on a ship. Because it could be used to calculate longitude, this clock helped Cook to accurately identify the location of many places. This was important on the ocean, where there were no landmarks to help sailors find their way.

On this voyage, Cook's ship was the *Resolution*. Another ship on the voyage was the *Adventure*. He sailed far south from England into the frigid waters around Antarctica. He and his men were the first people to travel south of the Antarctic Circle. Ice fields and freezing weather kept Cook from landing on the continent of Antarctica, but he sailed closer to it than anyone had dared to before.

Artists on Cook's voyages created pictures of what the explorers saw. Here, Cook's ship is seen among icebergs, near Antarctica. Men from the ship collected ice to melt for water.

Sailing Near Antarctica: From Captain Cook's Journal

"The clouds near the horizon were of a perfect snow whiteness and were difficult to be distinguished from the ice hills whose lofty [high] summits reached the clouds. The outer or northern edge of this immense ice field was composed of loose or broken ice so close packed together that nothing could enter it.… In this field we counted ninety-seven ice hills or mountains."

Cook felt certain that there was land under the ice. Though this was not the giant continent people expected him to find, he believed that this was the last continent that would be discovered in the Southern Hemisphere. He was right in both cases.

As Cook sailed closer to Antarctica, the terrible cold froze the ships' ropes and sails, making work nearly impossible. Surrounded by broken ice and towering icebergs, the two ships were in constant danger of being crushed. Cook tried several times to reach land but only got within one hundred miles of Antarctica's coast. The cold was too great, and Cook and his men were forced to give up.

Cook headed into the South Pacific, where he mapped many islands, including Tonga, Rapa Nui (Easter Island), Fiji, and the New Hebrides. But eventually, he turned back toward Antarctica, sailing all the rest of the way around the frozen continent before heading back to England.

Cook reached home in July 1775. This second voyage had taken more than three years and had covered seventy thousand miles.

This British map shows the routes of Cook's three voyages.

The Third Voyage

In the 1700s people still wondered whether there was a Northwest Passage, an ocean passage above North America connecting the Atlantic and Pacific Oceans. Cook was now forty-seven years old. He had spent nearly thirty years at sea. He was tired and his health was not good. Could he be asked to lead another expedition?

Cook understood how important the discovery of this passage would be to Britain. He said he would command this voyage and departed in July 1776.

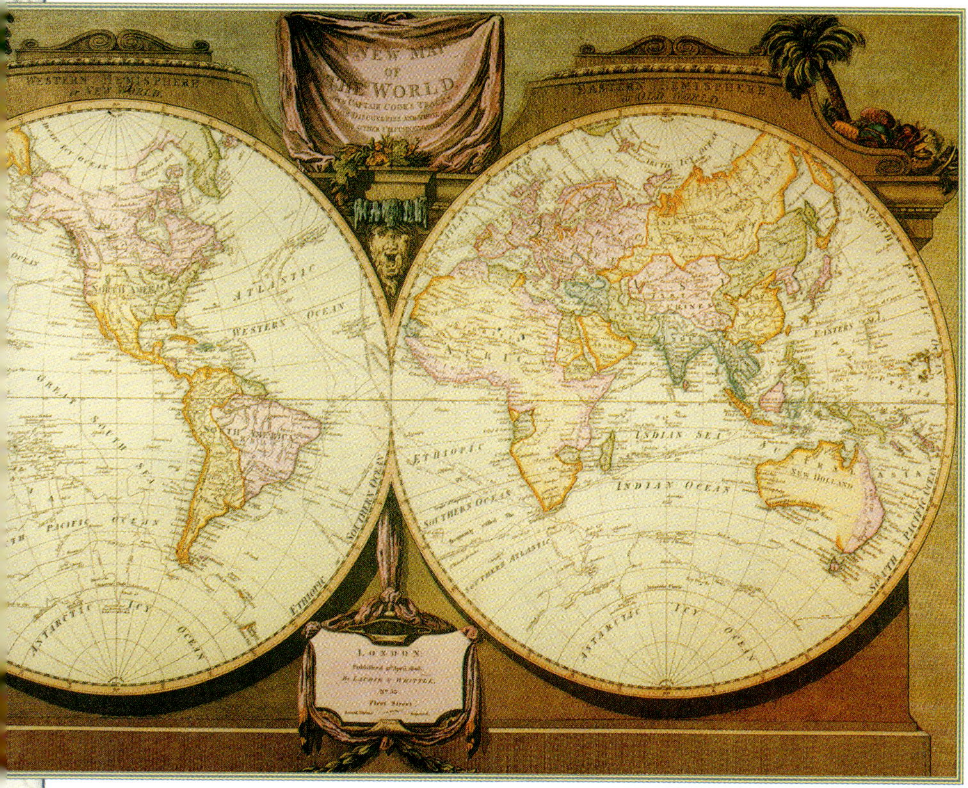

Cook again sailed on the *Resolution*, but on this voyage there was also a second ship, the *Discovery*. The two ships sailed south of Africa and into the Pacific Ocean. Traveling north, Cook found many new islands, including the Hawaiian Islands. When his ships stopped in Hawaii for supplies, the Hawaiians seemed friendly and happy to trade for food.

From Hawaii, Cook headed for North America. He explored the coast of what is now Oregon, Washington, and Alaska. Traveling up the coast, Cook and his crews continued to meet new people, many of them curious about the Europeans and eager to trade.

Cook sailed through the Aleutians, the string of islands in Alaska's far west, and into the Arctic Ocean.

This statue of James Cook stands in London, England.

Ahead of him were massive walls of ice. Cook got as close to the ice walls as he could. But there was no passage through to the Atlantic. Disappointed, Cook turned west. He charted part of the coast of Siberia, but winter was coming.

Cook felt that warm weather would be healthy for his crew, but he worried about the diseases his men might introduce into the islands. It was a difficult decision, but Cook and his crew returned to Hawaii.

The Hawaiians welcomed them at first, but tensions grew because of misunderstandings. Early in 1779 Cook again sailed north to look for a passage through the Arctic Ocean. But when one of the ships was damaged in a storm, he was forced to return to Hawaii. The Hawaiians were not happy about Cook's return. On February 14, 1779, several warriors met Cook on the beach and stabbed him to death. His saddened crew sailed back to England with the news.

James Cook is still honored today in England, as well as in many other parts of the world. He charted more of the Earth than anyone before him—and anyone since.

Glossary

equator the imaginary line that circles the center of Earth from east to west

frigid very cold

latitude the measurement of how far north or south of the equator a place is located

longitude the measurement of how far east or west of the prime meridian a place is located

Northern Hemisphere the half of Earth north of the equator

scurvy a disease caused by a lack of vitamin C

Southern Hemisphere the half of Earth south of the equator

voyage a journey by sea